AF571779

Why I Love My CAT

101 Dang Good Reasons

Ellen Patrick

ISBN 1-58173-401-8

This book was compiled with help from Virgil, Opal, and Floyd.

Jacket and text design by Miles G. Parsons
Printed in Italy

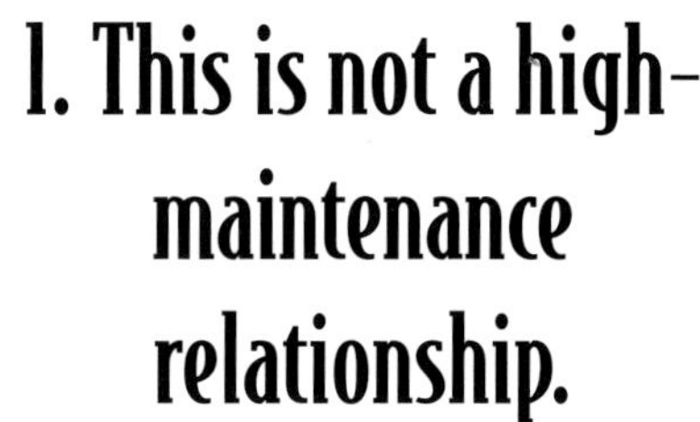

1. This is not a high-maintenance relationship.

2. At least someone in the house is limber.

3. Fur can be a very comforting thing.

4. No sappy sentimental mush.

5. There's nothing like a good purr after a long, hard day.

6. Understands every word I say.

7. Never argues.

8. Kicks varmint butt.

9. Can you say "above it all"?

10. Not lactose intolerant.

11. Excellent appreciation of ornithology.

12. Not afraid of heights.

13. Knows exactly what she wants.

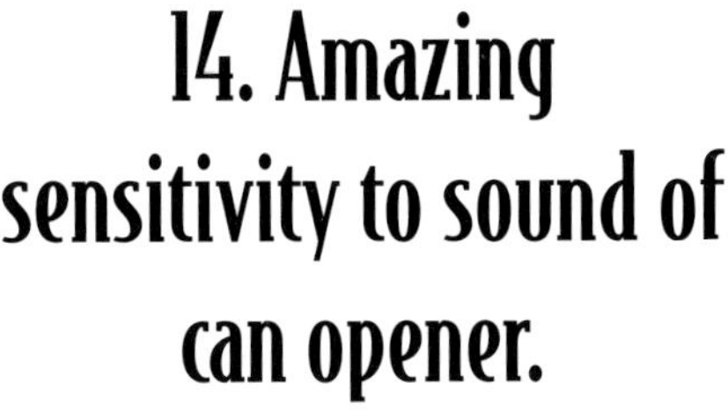

14. Amazing sensitivity to sound of can opener.

15. Does not sweat the small stuff.

16. Master at creative texturing of upholstery.

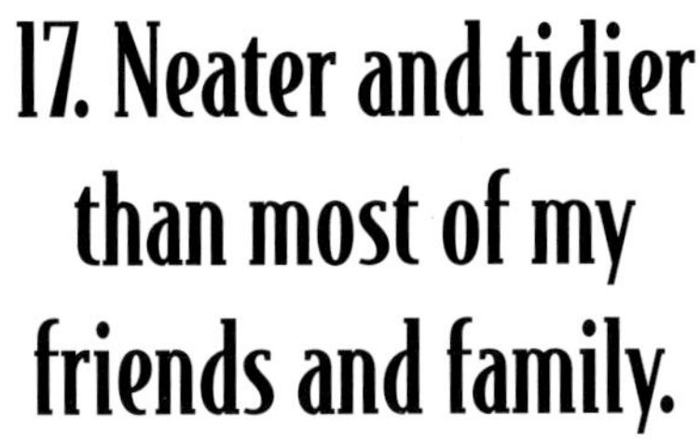

17. Neater and tidier than most of my friends and family.

18. Has a communication system all his own, called "tail-speak."

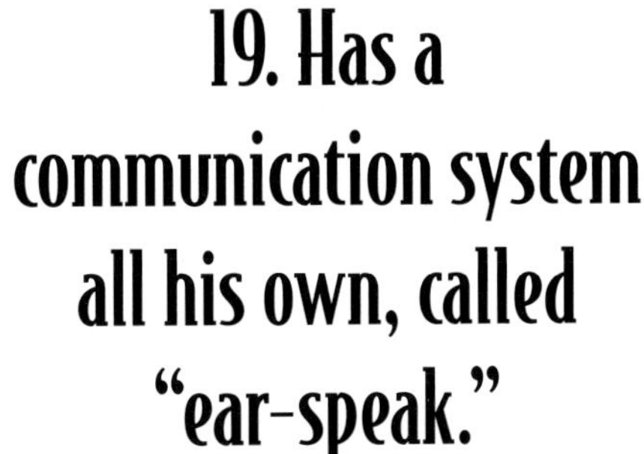

19. Has a communication system all his own, called "ear-speak."

20. Won't be bossed around by anyone.

21. Always seems to know exactly what I need.

22. Reminds me how much fun it is to play.

23. Always, always a lady or gentleman.

24. Protects his turf—
and mine.

25. Always forgives
my mistakes (after
letting me know how
dumb I can be).

26. Superb table manners.

27. Probably descended from royalty.

28. Never misses a lick.

---

29. Gets along with everyone—when she wants.

30. Has elevated napping to a high art.

31. Conveniently holds
down loose pillows
and cushions.

32. Has a healthy disrespect for veterinary medicine.

33. Helpfully carries small things from place to place around the house.

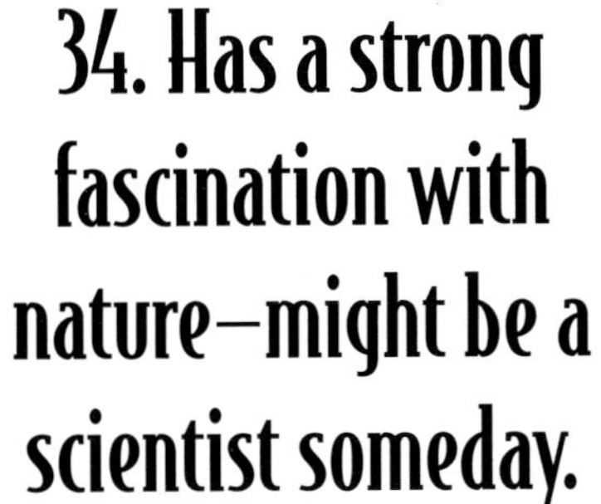

34. Has a strong fascination with nature—might be a scientist someday.

35. It's nice to see someone so comfortable in her own skin.

36. Has power, knows how to use it.

37. Easy to entertain.

38. Easy to bore.

39. Hard to fool.

40. No chance of an identity crisis.

41. Could do anything she wants to do—just chooses not to.

42. Does double duty as a heating pad.

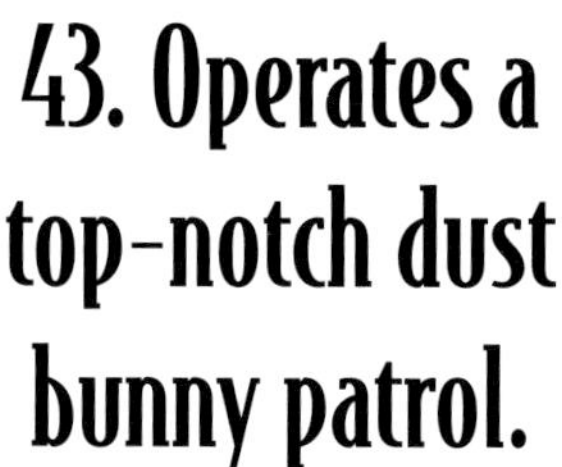

43. Operates a top-notch dust bunny patrol.

44. If I am really nice to him, gives me eye squeezes.

45. Biggest yawn in town.

46. Eats better than I do.

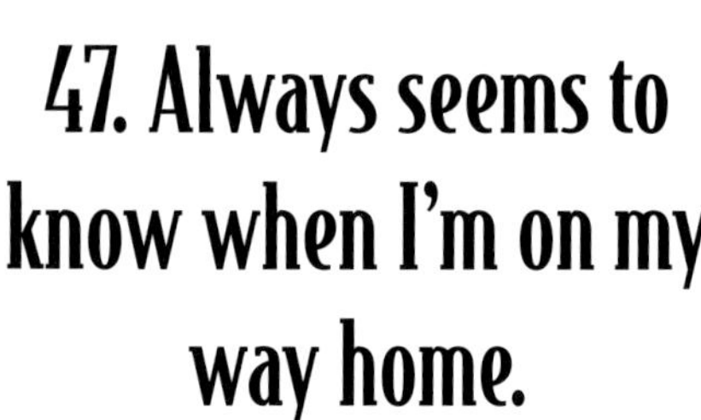

47. Always seems to know when I'm on my way home.

48. Can actually read my mind.

49. Knows 1001 different ways to meow.

50. Working on her master's degree in leisure studies.

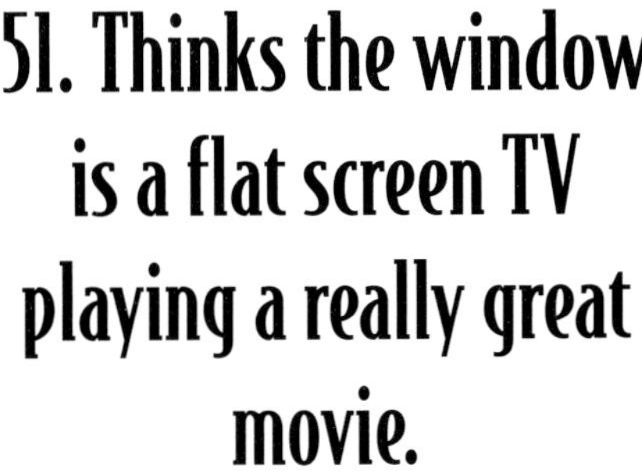

51. Thinks the window is a flat screen TV playing a really great movie.

52. Does not care what I look like.

53. Does not care how much money I make.

54. Does not care how much I weigh.

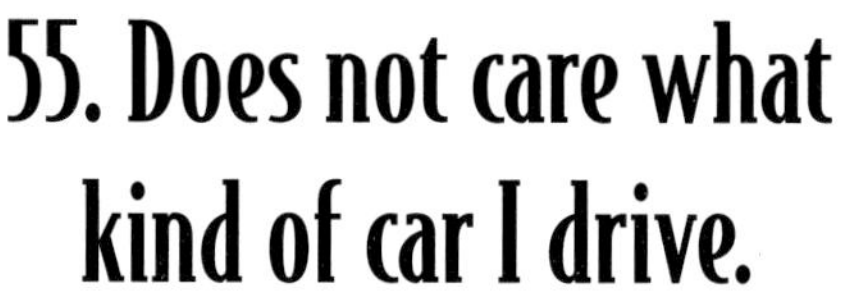

55. Does not care what kind of car I drive.

56. Does not care how young or old I am.

57. Cares more about tuna than anyone I know.

58. Actually smiles when I scratch that special spot.

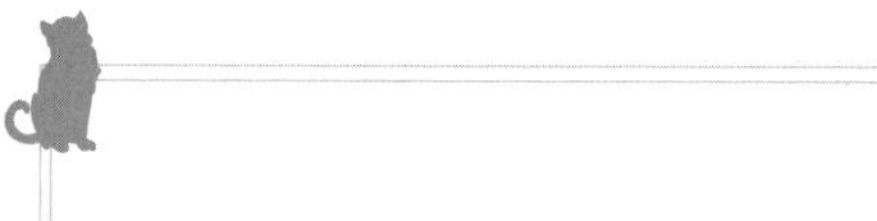

59. Wants the best for me, especially when it involves dairy products.

60. Has life in perspective.

61. Brings me the most interesting gifts.

62. Has the world on a string—literally.

63. Is thinking about opening a seafood restaurant.

64. Could be the smartest person I know.

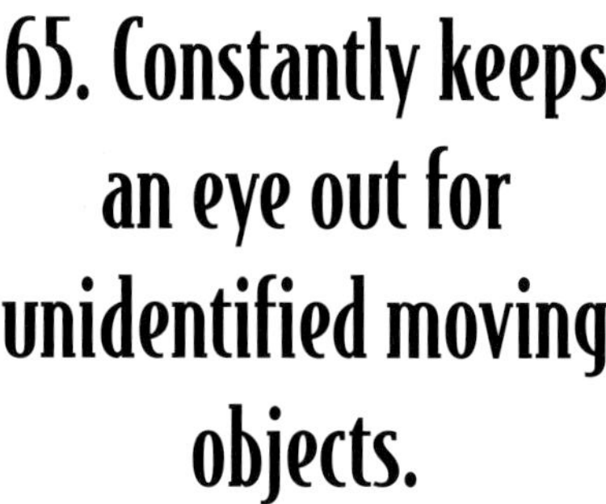

65. Constantly keeps an eye out for unidentified moving objects.

66. Leaps tall counters with a single bound.

67. Has a part-time job as a night watchman.

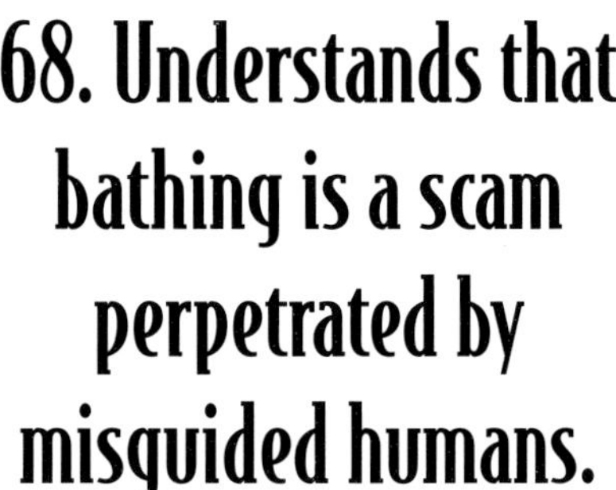

68. Understands that bathing is a scam perpetrated by misguided humans.

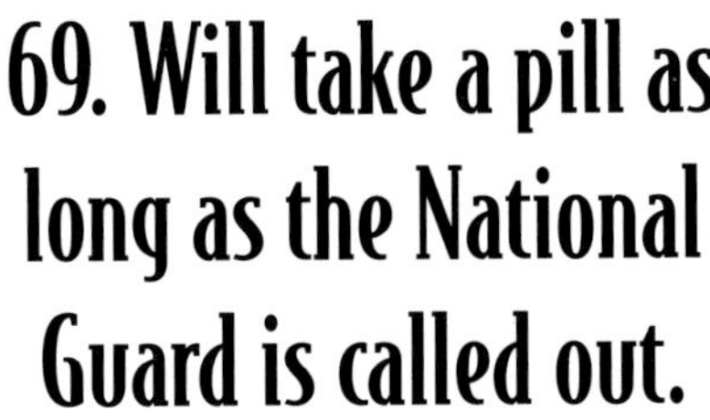

69. Will take a pill as long as the National Guard is called out.

70. Could do tricks, if only she wanted to.

71. Could do neurosurgery, if only he wanted to.

72. Knows all my secrets.

73. Keeps all my secrets.

77. Intelligent.

78. Discreet.

79. Tasteful.

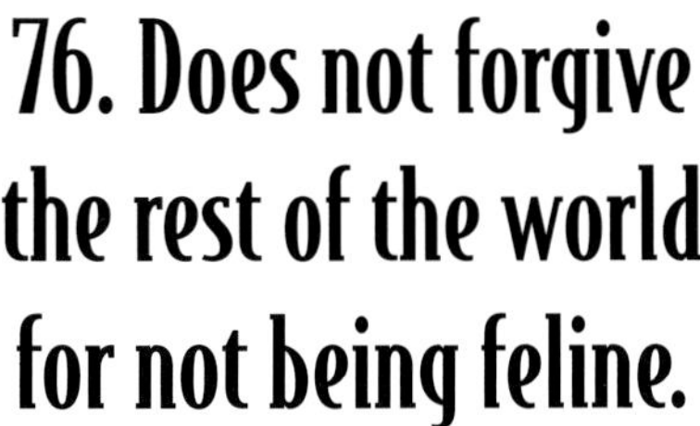

76. Does not forgive the rest of the world for not being feline.

75. Forgives me for not being feline.

74. No self-esteem problem here.

80. Dignified.

81. Discerning.

82. Patient.

83. Fun-loving.

84. Affectionate (more than she lets on).

85. No fool.

86. Always lands on his feet.

87. Cute toes.

88. Magical eyes.

89. A tail that can make you laugh out loud.

90. Sensitive.

91. Always in control of herself.

92. Always on top of things.

93. Reliable.

94. Frighteningly frisky.

95. 100% effective in eliminating risk of loneliness.

96. 100% effective in eliminating risk of boredom.

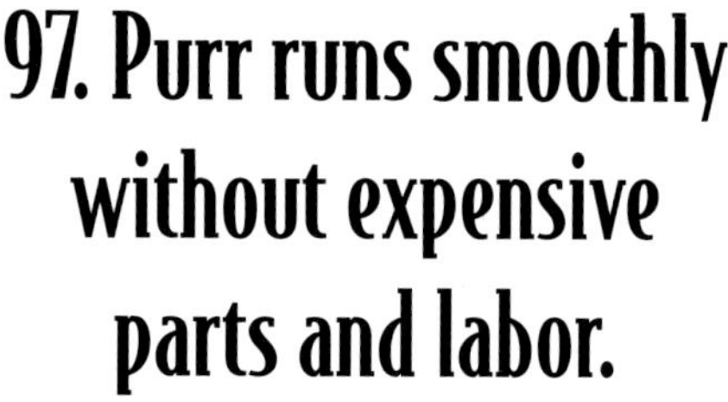

97. Purr runs smoothly without expensive parts and labor.

98. Just plain sweet.

99. This is the only fur coat I'll ever need.

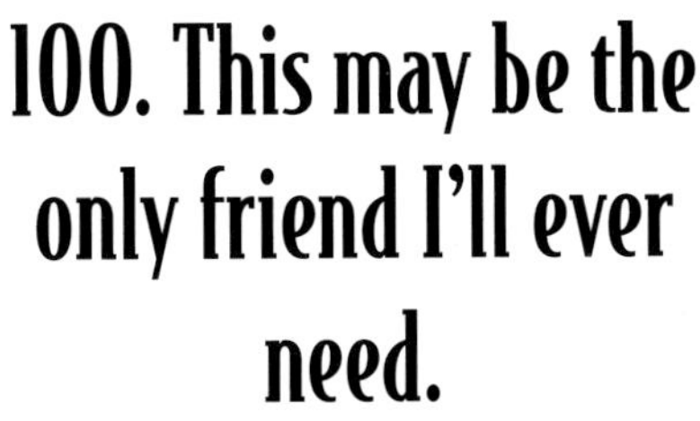

100. This may be the only friend I'll ever need.

101. Out of all the humans on earth, my cat picked me.